D1133783

Your Life is a Masterpiece

Poems by

Rebecca Folsom

Edited by Karen Horan
Author photo by John Mueller
Cover design by Celeste Krenz

Published by
Kalmia Publishing
Sunshine Productions
PO Box 1073
Boulder, CO 80306
www.rebeccafolsom.com

For the curious who lift the covers off and have the
courage to live in the truth of themselves.

Also by Rebecca Folsom:

Poetry:
    Sliver

Music:
    Welcome Home

    Many Miles

    Across the Sky

    Ruby, Live at the Velvet

    Shine

    Water on Stone

Visit www.rebeccafolsom.com for touring schedule, booking information, workshop offerings, and more.

Contents

Acknowledgements

So many people went into the creation of this book. Some signed on directly and specifically with a task in mind, and others without knowing it, influenced its creation by a word, a deed, a story, or by individual essence of character. My gratitude to you all is larger than words. Big thanks to all of humanity for our shared struggles and joys; to nature for her refuge, healing, and reflections of power and beauty, to the humbling power of death, and to the incredible force running through everything that we call life, god, spirit, essence. There are particular individuals that carry this life force with such an inspiring mixture of grace, grit, perseverance, patience, kindness, and humor that it is to you I dedicate this work and offer immense gratitude!

Reta Lawler, what an absolute gift you are! Thank you for your steady spirit and vast love. My sister Amy Jacquemard, how did we get so lucky to share an entire lifetime with each other? You are a constant source of comfort, clarity, and fun. My mother Margaret Clough, thank you for the gift of life, your enduring love, and your delight in hearing the poems du jour as they were written daily! My brothers John Scott Clough and Mike Clough for your unending loyalty and support as only brothers can. My sister Kathy for your love. My dad John Clough for your willingness to heal with me and rediscover the love that was never truly lost. Myrtle and Bill Lyle for lighting the way on how to live fully. Jim Jacquemard, Sandy Clough, Davis and Kathy Folsom for your hands-on help and support from figuring out laptops to setting up concerts and selling CDs; I am immensely grateful. Nicole Jacquemard, Genevieve, Jeremy, Jake, and Sienna Clough for your tender hearts and incredible potential. Susy, Jonathan, and Laura Clough for the doors opened and the love shared. Each individual in the huge and brilliant Clough and Folsom families, you are all so special.

Karen Horan for your immeasurable support, your intelligence, your fiery nature, and your deep understanding of what the books wanted to say. Your editing and feedback were invaluable. To Americo, Gayle, and Arilu Yabar for the essence of who you are, how you help reassemble people towards trust and love, and the dedication of your work. Denise Townsend for the deep friendship shared, twins on the same path. The Goddesses - Denise Wissman, Alyson Bell, Margaret Clough, Karen Horan, Marla Konowitch, Leanne Soucek, Denise Maierhofer - what a magic circle of kindness, kick-buttness, and good intent. Extra thanks to Alyson Bell for your perseverance, good will, and holding the office together so that I have time to write. Chris Malley, Celeste Krenz, Liz Barnez, and Sally Barris for your love of music and writing, and all the fun we have sharing it with the world. Tom Kimmel for all of your help and your inspirational work, and Robyn for putting together such a fine meeting of poetry and song at your home. Joe Calloway for the bright light and enthusiasm you shine on possibility. Jan Scarbrough for your shared experience. Audrey Alton for being a gem, thank you for welcoming me and the friendship shared.

To Michael Young, Dr. Anne Mattson and whole staff, Dr. Larry Eckstien, Dr. David Thayer, Anna Chitty, Denise Wissman, Denise Townsend for your expertise and kind work. To the entire staff at Vic's Coffee shop for your daily kindness.

To my stepson, Nathan Folsom, you continue to be an inspiration for the gentleness with which you live. It has been an honor to share in the passion for the arts with you. To my stepdaughter Julie Faulkner for the goodness in the depth of your being, for the joy you have brought into the world with your beautiful children. My grandchildren Maia and Jackson Faulkner for your shining, shining spirits! Maia, you were an important part of *Sliver*, the very first poem written. You both make my heart smile so wide it hurts sometimes. And, to Roger Folsom, my love, my best friend, my most intimate confidante. Your support, love, humor, and practical wisdom have been a touchstone for so many years. Thank you, dear friend, for who you are!

And, to you dear reader, thank you for listening, for seeking, and for being yourself.

Introduction

I hadn't planned on writing a poetry book, let alone two. Even when I had six journals with pages full of what I called "The Poem du Jour" I still did not think I was writing a book. I am a songwriter by trade and for years have been committed to the craft of weaving lyric, melody, and arrangement into song. I didn't see these books coming, and that is an important piece of their magic. Being a professional, having released numerous recordings and performed thousands of public shows, I had opened myself to (if not sought) reviews from critics and weekly feedback from audiences. I hadn't realized that over time I developed a filter in my writing that was tempering how I expressed myself, subtly checking how to present an idea, how it would perform and be best received by the public. As I wrote these poems, I never thought they would be read by the public, so without knowing, I bypassed the professional filter.

These writings happened daily for a little over a year in a number of different locations, but mostly in a favorite local café where I felt at home drifting on the chatter and hum of the humanity there. I love these bohemian places where people take the time to come together and connect with each other, to share food and drink, and exchange ideas.

These poems came on the heels of a fundamental letting go that involved a mandatory shift in the way I approached my daily life. I slowed my momentum to a stop. While this stop opened up and gifted beautiful new perspectives, a way of moving with depth rather than speed, it was disorienting to almost all my sense of meaning and identity. My situation demanded that I prune my way of operating in the world to only what felt true to me, which at first seemed like a good old house cleaning, throwing out old beliefs, and discarding limited ways of functioning. As the process continued to unfold, and my sense of self was pared down to so excruciatingly and blissfully little, I felt I could be thread through the eye of a small needle. It is within the essence of this place that *Sliver* and *Your Life is a Masterpiece* were born.

At the time, the writing of the poems felt like a daily meditative practice, a thread that helped me hold to my grip of the world. Holding onto my sanity by a thread has new meaning! Then, as obviously as the poems had begun, they slowly trickled to an end. It was then apparent that two books had been written. As a focused goal-oriented "doer" this was a very backwards way of creating something. I am deeply grateful to this process and the kind and masterful friends who helped me navigate its passage. I am oddly humbled and strengthened by it, and I am pleased that the writings decided to reveal themselves at this time, so that what has felt like such a gift in change in perspective can be shared with you.

I hope that these poems give you something that you need—awakening, enlivening, uplifting, freedom, compassion, laughter, connectedness, strength, balance, comfort, inspiration, peace. May we know the value of our truth and our kindness, for within the sliver of who we are, how humbly and majestically we create the masterpiece of our lives.

– Rebecca

Your Life is a Masterpiece

Take Back Your Power

First Day

Stepping slowly into the water,
a strong heart
quivers at a simple risk.

What is it to reach out,
step in,
initiating
with a vulnerable heart,
without agenda but deeply invested,
listening to the subtle currents
and, for everyone's sake, letting go?
To let the unfolding of life
touch me back
with its tragic suffering,
release, and laughter,
its untamable complexity?

The humor in how I don't fit,
the wrong clothes for the occasion,
doing this thing out of character,
awkward social interaction,
crashing and tumbling,
my inner walls collapsing.
This place will never feel perfect,
and yet, from a larger perspective,
it is refreshingly perfect.

One small act, a couple toes in the water…

A Symbol of Power

No words
only senses and symbols.

You reach a point
during the intensity of the ride
when you're no longer talking.
There is just the smell of fur flying
heaving sides and spitting nostrils,
sweat through jeans
where thighs meet rib cage in and out.

This animal is doing its own dance.

I am holding to it,
leaving the ground,
the inevitable return,
whole body shaking loose,
spine like a slinky.

If I slow down time,
it becomes graceful instead of jarring.

How I love and am wary of this beast,
a symbol of power.
How I love myself and my mastery,
knowing,
like when you look in the eyes
of somcone about to win,
this time
you will not throw me.

It Can Be Done with Love

Even the most difficult tasks can be done with love.
When it comes to the grist, the rubbing,
the pearl making of our souls,
we have an important choice:
    to be born into the moment with anger and fear, or
    to be born with awe and kindness.

Magic Words

Please.
After you.
I'm sorry.
I don't know.
What do you need?
What can I do?
Stop it.
I didn't do it.
I did it.
Thank you.

All magic words.
And, with any magic,
it is best to use mindfully, carefully.

As children we learn the effectiveness
of using these words,
different keys to function and get what we need.

Sometimes a key works so well;
we think it will work for everything.
Repeat any of these words over and over
and listen to how desperate they become:

Please, please, please, please, please, please, please…
After you, after you, after you, after you, after you…
I'm sorry, I'm sorry, I'm sorry, I'm sorry, I'm sorry…
"Thank you" is the only one that
holds up in repetition.

But, don't be fooled by its perceived grace,
for after receiving an injurious slap in the face,
the less beautiful "stop it" is of more value
than a million "thank yous."

Delicate Ecosystem

I am tired
of the maintenance of living.

By addressing the hold I've had on life,
all the myriad of ways that I have clung to survival,
my grip has finally loosened,
and what I find here
is exhaustion.
Trauma once compressed,
encapsulated inside,
floods its toxicity out
into the rivers of my blood,
rewiring my synaptic spark,
affecting the landscape of skin and tissue;
all intelligent systems
doing their part to clear
dis-ease from my delicate ecosystem.

Peace, freedom, love—
all concepts I hold to like a raft
in this undoing.
I have lost so much in this flooding,
strength, identity, a reference to interface
with the world.
And, I hold to my vision
of the future,
whispering with what must be relentless kindness
to let go and know
that what is left
will be exactly
what is needed.

Not Doing

Let yourself down
into not doing.
Cross over the intimidating barbed wire fence
any way you can.

Over time,
if you make a habit of it,
the wire becomes bent into opening,
and the maneuver can be done with grace,
not a scratch,
and you're in greener pastures,
open sky lifting
the seriousness of time
fading into wisps of feathered clouds
and contemplation billowing.

Let go of what the world thinks of you
and reflect on the world.

So much can be lost in our accomplishing,
our social engagement,
focus designed for covering rapid ground,
highly valued.
But, what of the days that beckon
to rest,
to take the blinders off,
and slow the step
and feel
moist dirt
warm from the sun's kiss.

Spring grass swathed in
colors it dresses in
only once a year,

clear-throated vigorous birds,
so small, heralding morning songs,
the change in one's own skin
as it opens and softens,
encouraged by spring's
cascading, tumbling
"tag, you're it" unfoldment.

How many seasons
have you engaged in,
slowed down enough
to truly meet?

Allow yourself to listen
to the magic of not doing.
It has such a different voice.
Try not to be scared off
by the spaciousness.
Allow yourself to feel
life touch you back,
and for this moment receive
what is here.

EnCourage

EnCourage:
a word of relationship.
Isn't it nice to be encouraged?
Filled with, engaged in, incited to courage?

When you drop the self pity
and look your challenges straight in the eye,
are they not filled
with information about what to do next?

That is where courage steps in.

Like a lion, courage joins you,
becomes an ally if you
really let yourself partner with it.

Hands on soft fur,
vigorous patting on strong rib cage,
a healthy appreciation
for the wild, dignified roar.

Meet your life with courage.
Expect a few battles,
a few moments of bared teeth,
to protect the integrity of your dream.
Run full stride and let yourself be strong.

And, know that sometimes it takes
great courage to rest,
panting, melting in the sun,
with your endurance having made you ready

to spring to life at a moment's notice
and meet what lies before you.

Encourage yourself.

Accept it from every source.
Gather it. Know its value.

For a life lived in the wild
demands for your survival
absolute engagement,
acting on what is next
without knowing outcomes.

Take Back Your Power

Listen to the heartbeat of the world
and take back your power.

Of course you are rejecting the status quo;
your body cannot swallow it anymore.
Embrace your sweet, unique life,
unfolding every moment into the unknown.

Do not be swayed
by persuasions and demands,
or the more insidious,
pious expectation
of your behavior.
Choose your own course
wisely or unwisely,
but stay awake and choose.

Listen to the heartbeat of the earth.
Align with what you are made of
and let go into your own creation.
The time will be right
to offer the thousand-petaled gift
effortlessly,
being yourself.

Your Life is a Masterpiece

The Precipice

Perfect Undoing

Everything was going so well.
Sights clear.
Breath steady.
Everything lined up.

Then, life in its unwieldy exuberance
came dancing in,
tumbled over my settings,
disconnected my wires,
and undid my fine tuning.

How this happens again and again,
wanting something solid
to stay comfortable.

Then, chaos shows up,
moves the furniture,
reveals all the unswept corners,
exposes the dirt,
and, like a tornado, airs out the place.

If we can stay light,
this unsettling
lifts us into new places
where our safe thinking never lets us go.

Kiss life for how it stirs you!

For delivered on its unpredictable winds
again and again
is the gift
of your perfect undoing.

My Trip through the Desert

I was stuck in a world view.
I was operating out of "not enough,"
riding through my days at full throttle,
on my toes, pushing ahead,
making up for what I lacked inside
by accomplishing more, covering more ground.
Then disaster struck…

and I broke down.

Not careening out of control like times in the past,
with a quick regrouping and back on track,
but a slow and thorough stopping,
leaving me alone on the side of the road
in the desert.

I checked my systems.
I kicked and screamed.
I cried out for help.
And then I listened…

It is so quiet in the desert.

At first it felt like nothing was there,
but in time, I became more sensitive,
and I could hear
a lizard move from yards away.
I could tell
how the sun's angle at different
times in the day brought out
different smells—
sage, dust, valuable moisture
from a river far away.

And, when the hawks flew overhead
the sound of their feathers
pressing against the sky
was almost deafening.

In this place, I have vacillated between
astounding awe and utter boredom.
In the stream of thoughts that slowed to a trickle,
to a drop, one remaining was…

"As beautiful as this is,
how I yearn for the breadth of the road."

But, time is different in the desert,
and my learning to wait
took much longer that I thought.
My vehicle could not be patched together again.
It had to be fully and completely discarded,
a goodbye filled with sadness, relief,
and complete confusion as how to proceed.

Disorientation is a right of passage,
an initiation in itself.
Gradually, inspiring movement to begin again,
using my longing as a compass,
I found it best to move slowly.

Frankly, I am amazed how moving
at this pace, my impact more subtle,
harmonious within the design of things,
brings so much to me.

And, sitting in this seat
of the silent, roaring miraculous now,

I am no longer driven by not enough,
no longer lost in isolating and speeding.
I am found
calm, grateful, trusting in synchronicity.
And, now my life is moved…

by love.

The Precipice

Standing on the precipice,
I hesitate,
I listen,
I feel some resistance.

Fear.

But my whole being knows
this is where I am supposed to go.
Let go of all past expectations
and definitions.

How deep, how shallow?
How warm, how cold?
How long will I drop?

The dive is imperative.

I remind myself that I am not
the same person standing on these cliffs.
My mastery has grown.

Trust.
Trust the trajectory.
Trust the real meeting.

Skin to stone, to air, to water,
propelled by love,
always propelled by love
when living fluidly
in the face of not knowing,
always propelled by love.

I Went Looking

I went looking for the old stone
that I threw in the river when letting go
was the right thing to do.

Churning, bubbling in swirls,
the old turns to new.

I went looking, but I wasn't prepared.
I had to hold on to too many parts of myself.
One would drop.
I would grab it and let go of another,
repeating until I was frantic
and lost my balance.

That's when my keys fell.

I was afraid the current would take them
and leave me stranded.
They fell to the bottom, resting on the stones.
What a picture, looking at those keys underwater,
like a dream I had,
deciding to dive in or not,
wondering how cold it would feel.

I reached in and grabbed them back
from the other side.
The water was still too fast,
and I am not prepared, yet.
I will come back, when the water is lower
and the timing is right.

Prelude to the Truth is Always Better

There used to be so many reasons;
There used to be so many systems;
There used to be so many strategies of defense
        supporting this fortress.

What wordless terror has been found
behind these stones, in these dark corners
where truth
was cloaked
walking backward to exact time and place,
when the deal was made to abandon self.

What desperate circumstance has pressed so hard that
we are found bartering our souls?
Held hostage by deception
carrying a slow costly ransom,
we wait until we are able to gather about us
all remaining resources,
pull out all fearlessness, refuse all conditioning,
        and
            storm the castle.

When you storm the castle
all hell breaks loose and leaves your body.

The Truth is Always Better

Have you noticed?
        In every situation in life
the truth is always better,
        always a perfect fit
            that unlocks the magic
        and moves dreams into reality.

Resistance

Let Your Flaws Be

Let your flaws be the passageway
to your soft heart.
Let your flaws be the sharp knife
that sets you free
from any tight packaging.

Let your flaws be
the zipper, the buttons, the fraying seam you rip
to loosen up.
Let them be the weathered crack in the wall
that lets in a sliver of light, a breath of fresh air,
when the doors of your heart
have been locked for too long.

Let your flaws be
the incision on your tender skin
that opens you
only to remove what has been ailing you
from holding yourself together for so long.

Let your flaws be
the fissure that allows
your deepest well of being to spring forth,
quenching the thirst
of true connection for yourself and
everyone around you.

Satiated we sit at the table
open, undone, a few scars, a few loose edges.
Are we not full of delight
relaxing here in the beauty of our natural state?

Give Up

Give up
defending yourself.
Listen
to what the "other" outside has to say.

Choose it or leave it,
but do not brace
your heart.

Let go your fists
and open
to the constant dialog
unweaving and unwinding
your weary sense of self.

Cry.
Let the tears
melt your walls
so the love that you are
shines through.

Laugh until you shatter
the serious façade.

And embrace,
embrace
this precious life
that is yours
alone.

Your Yes

Go the way you want to go.
Put your hand up, palm out,
and stop the ways you do not want to go,
with no apologies.
It can be done with grace and kindness,
with a bow and well wishes.
Slide into your true direction.
Slip into something more comfortable.

Are you going to waste your valuable time
sitting at a table you have no business being at,
idling away precious hours
out of politeness?
This is a bardo state of the living.

Consider the alternative.

If you follow your "yes"
and follow through by honoring what is a "no",
what creative magic lies waiting
in your every next step.

Choosing to steer from the heart,
with the whole body as informant,
you become synchronized
within yourself.
And, because *there is no separation*,
all of life
hums, rattles, and rolls
in alignment with you.

Unfettered by ties that bind
your "yes" becomes the key,
a perfect fit

to the universe,
and the soul aim
becomes one,
joined, powerful, and
subtly balanced within the truth of your momentary
choices.

Your "yes" introduces your individual self
over and over again
in ecstatic embrace
to "all that is".

The Missing Piece

Sweet fire.
The womb.
A memory of my mother's kiln.
The missing piece fitting
perfectly at top
and the vehicle of creation all comes together.

To come this far in rebuilding
and to fit the last piece
has its own challenge.
I am aware that this sliver
must be impeccably placed.
I'm moved by power,
the truth unfolding,
and simultaneously,
terrified by the movement of power.
It is always annihilation of the ego
that terrifies.
In embracing my ultimate demise
at any moment,
it is so much easier
to let go
into the flashing current
of power's design.
The eagle is large,
overwhelming to the mind.
Is the practice then
to dissolve my boundaries
by dying to all things,
so that I can truly live?

Yesterday
what was asked of me
in answer

to my bid for freedom – the requirements –
unbound me so quickly.
The speed had me spinning,
dizzy, nauseous,
unable to see clearly
or function,
unleashed
into the spaciousness of the eagle.
What was ground
became the deepest of canyons
untied, released off the edge,
no up or down,
disoriented to say the least.
The spinning,
when I relax into it,
takes on its own grace
and becomes more like a whipping boomerang.
I felt my edges press
into the air,
and as boomerangs do,
I returned.

My breath inside of me now,
I found my footing
by taking only
the next right step.
And, as I walk
at the edge of this cliff,
beautiful views soothe me,
changing winds alert and cleanse me.
Gliding raven reminds me
the missing piece will come to me.

I will take the next right step
and sometimes that step…

is right over the edge.

Know Yourself

Know yourself.
What does home look like
as you carry it these many miles
of a lifetime?

Know yourself.
Where is center?
How far can you lean
without toppling over?

Know yourself.
In this sea of bi-ways and habitations,
where do I end
and you begin?

Know yourself.
How are your reserves
and where did the leaking occur?

Know yourself
so that when something is given to you,
you know it came from another's home
cultivated and tended,
then lovingly offered.

Know yourself
so that you know without a doubt
what your garden offers
and you give without regret,
knowing the wealth of being
always replenishes upon itself.

Some Guests

Doubt is a powerful bedfellow.
Innocent enough at first glance,
it appears natural
that he is at the party.

Maybe it is even smart
that he is there
to keep you safe,
keep an eye out for you.

Not a big fellow, but he can grow.

And, when doubt gets going,
jealousy, fear, sadness, and anger
are quick to huddle and
take over the room.

And, where does that leave you?

Be careful who you invite into your home,
for some guests are not what they appear.

Resistance

Resistance,
something to get over we are taught.

But resistance in itself has so much to teach.

Resistance is a voice
telling us other truths.
It isn't bad, as in good or bad.
It is a force,
the natural push and pull
of different directions.

When you feel resistance
settle into the pressure.
What is the dissonant movement?
Where is your truth aligned, and
what is pulling on it?

Each moment is an opportunity
to redefine and refine yourself.
How do you wish to assemble?

See resistance for what it is:
You talking to you.
No need to fight yourself or the world.
Make your choices
and listen.

If the answers smile,
reflected in your
peace, your passion, your curiosity, your ecstasy,
then you have chosen well.

If your choices dull you

then do not hesitate:
cut your way out.
Run the other way,
and thank resistance
for making of you
the sharp knife,
cutting through what is extraneous,
living on the edge of life.

Let Go into the Fall

Let Go into the Fall

Leap
and look.
Assemble yourself
and dissolve.
Let go your holding, rest your eyes.
Let the experience come to you.

It is the nature of gravity
to pull you toward a meeting point.
Enjoy the flight.

If you let go into the fall
the process of life brushing through you,
and let experience touch you deeply,
it gets under your skin.
Holding loosens and flutters away,
taking layers, pieces, heavy limbs,
and releases them like party favors
into catapulting little birds amidst
the floating cinder and ash.

If you let go into the fall
and let it loosen you up
what was your pain, transformed in the drop,
becomes the Phoenix
rising as your gift
to the healing of the world.

If on the trip
you don't take it lightly,
the meeting point is sure.

Sometimes we would rather
hit hard for the promise of surety.
And, dusting ourselves off yet again,
we say "Best to avoid those high places."

But, the inner compass is magnetized
to the path.
And, we are drawn over and over
to the journey that offers us freedom,
stripping us of everything unessential,
until we are left lightly
only as hearts with wings.

River that Sings

Sweet delight.
Oh, to be in the river that sings.
Effortless movement,
no longer moored with borrowed rope,
to be streaming
towards heart's desire,
to be living the dream,
and the dream living you,
a perfect fit
and manifesting is easy.

Do not resist yourself.
What is your truth?
You are god speaking.
Why would you distort
the purity of creation running through you?

For smaller minds?
They stand at the river's edge
afraid of the current, watching while you laugh,
yelling "how can you be so selfish?"

Fluidity can look inconsistent
if your eyes are not fully open,
still holding to blinders
of commitment and owing.

But look deeper.
A whole new world reveals itself,
and the constancy of love and delight
fills everything,
no strings attached.

What Is, No More, No Less

I want to fear nothing in life.

When I relax into the power point of
"What is,
No more, No less,"
there is no worry
and no need for manipulation.

There is in its place a relaxed stability,
for there is no constructed reality,
no lies told or insinuated,
no house of cards begging to be blown down.

"What is,
No More, No less"
a mantra repeating, reminding,
one point to steady myself around.

"What is,
No more, No less"
is very personal.
Think how we endlessly push ourselves,
wasting precious creative energy,
measuring,
we are too much, we are not enough.

Infinite discontent,
soul spilling
as endless dripping
sometimes in torrents.

What if we stopped the leak

and swaddled ourselves in self love?
As is!

Even in the face of the people
we want to impress most,
we hold to that love
with no betrayal.
What magic is possible
from such a true foundation
in celebration,
open hearted,
connected to infinite possibilities
from right where you are.

You Are the Key

Begin simply, anywhere,
at home, inside yourself,
some disassembly required.
Call upon the wind and have it comb stale thinking
from your mind.
Allow the earth to commune with your feet,
newly bare.
Receive the river and let it sieve away any debris
from your strong heart.

You are the key
and resting is a vital piece
in the coming and going
of making your way in the world.

We are invited to jump off the wheel
made up of speed and jockeying for position,
asking natural questions:
What is of value? What is of purpose?

Shall we assemble ourselves for greatness,
neither shrinking from our natural beauty
nor pushing and posturing out of fear?
To become a centerpoint
of what truly is,
by being true to who you are,
slipping into synchronicity,
it is possible to relax into a perfect fit.

The world needs
to see itself through your eyes.
Your vision is the eye of the storm,
opening within you the power
to change the daily momentum,

dissipating destruction
spreading peaceful, creative solutions.

You are the key
that frees the system
and sets into motion a new balance,
a dynamic equilibrium.
In the turning,
know your value.
What do you have to offer?
No more, no less.

You are the key
and within you lies the opportunity
to open the door
and become the gracious host
of infinite possibilities.

No Resistance

No Resistance.
How deep does the impact of that go?

Truly no resistance,
no contorting your face,
your body,
your words,
your mood
around what should be,
a deep relaxing
into what is.

Today, I think about the subtle infiltration
of control,
bracing, managing, second guessing.
Taking things personally
is wrapped in
self preservation,
preservation of a self
destined to perish.

To relax into death is the ultimate
No Resistance,
a movement each of us will make,
gracefully or not.

Why not let go today,
every moment of living matched
by dying to every moment,
releasing the limitations of our fear?

Let yourself be fluid.
Set yourself free on the subtle power
of moving tides.

Breathing Space

Be patient, breathe.

Impatience is so often tied to lack of trust.

Breathing space…

In the gap where either
inspiration or expiration occurs,
there is an inclination
to grasp for what inspires and
an aversion toward what expires.

In breathing space

who knows which way it will go,
but we do know both are needed,
and expiration must occur
for inspiration to be possible.

Be patient, breathe.

Let go into the unstoppable movement
of in and out.

If you are stuck, ask your body
which way you are holding.

Are your beautiful lungs full or empty?

Are you in need of in breath,

inspiration,

taking in life,

receiving?

Or,

are you in need of out breath,

expiration,

giving away,

letting go of cluttered life?

Take deeply from the river,
but do not forget
to remain in synchronicity
with natural flow,
you must throw everything back
that has no life force left for you.

And, remember, mirrored in perfect balance
to our miraculous first breath

that our last movement here,

one of great power,

will be expiration.

Death as Advisor

Die a Little Everyday

Let go.

In every response, how much is grasping
to not lose ground, to hold to survival,
to fight any kind of break down or decay?

Your life is fragile.

And, said without morbidity but in actuality,
your life was doomed from the start.

Why not let go
and, true to form, die a little everyday?

Shed the skin of all your holding.
Protect less.
The words you use to defend:
Throw them to the wind.

And in the silence left,
hear with aching sweetness
the remaining beats
of your uncovered heart.

Death as Advisor

I spend too much time wrestling
with the "right" thing to do.

Time spends itself on us,
and Death stands at our shoulder
watching what we do.
Death, the only one
that knows the bottom line
of our bank account.

Most days I'm oblivious,
spending, spending, spending.
Sometimes a sigh that opens to
            the sky,
                    a landscape,
                            a human heart,
                                    open eyes,
then back to spending.

Like the digital machine
that tallies the national deficit,
numbers flying,
shocking how fast it goes,
like drops of water,
a constant stream of pennies.

"Oh, it's just a penny."
The moment is so small,
we forget its worth.

But Death doesn't forget.
It holds us accountable

for all of those moments
streaming into a life.

I am tired of wrestling
with myself,
over doing the "right" thing,
wasting myself on second guessing.

When I have stillness enough
to stop,
to look up from the tangled mess of life
and converse with death,
immediately there is a wordless message that yells:

"Get on with it."

"Make your choices and move."

Death sees what a vessel I am,
values my capabilities,
and with patience
that lasts like an in-breath into eternity…
Death waits for me.

We All Stand at the Precipice

All this reflection of death.

The more I go into it
the more it reveals life
reverberating, pristine, fleeting,
clear definitions
on my direction
and what is a waste of savoring precious time.

We all stand at the precipice.

How can the water be so far below
and yet lapping at my feet as
I climb higher on these cliffs?

Death is surrounded by questions and mystery,
moated by the endless sacred lake and rising fog.
Beyond picturesque,
it is simultaneously crisp and soft here.
Sun setting, coloring the sky
reflected on the water's surface,
I hold to a little piece of dry rock.
I see myself in the clouds,
realize I am dreaming,
and awake into the freedom of consciousness.
Heart beating loudly, echoing
against this profoundly
beautiful backdrop of power and silence…

I jump.

Flow and the Starfish

Flow is easy
when the current is just right, a happy ride.

But, when the water recedes
and we are left like starfish flopping,
struggling to return to sea,
surrendering finally,
drying in the sand,
we wonder what went wrong,
why have we been forsaken.

Even if we remember that the tide does return,
will it be in time?
What we call self might die here,
this time thrown so far from the sea.

But, that is the nature of flow,
so much bigger than the small forms
we identify with.

Ebbing,
filling, flooding,
drying,
dying,
out of control.

If you stretch your mind
into the vastness,
and little by little
begin to grasp
the truth of no separation,

you no longer need to hold on,
for no matter where flow takes you,
you are always at home,
at sea,
in the sand,
as dust.

Flow is change and
change is intelligent evolution.

Let go into the receding,
the flooding,
the birthing, the dying.
Rejoice in the constant turning,

and gracefully, gracefully
embody and relinquish your form
in every awakened moment.

This Transformation is Taking a Long Time

I am so tired of not being what I want to be.
I am stuck and angry and talking to myself
about what looks like not following through,
wondering maybe it's just that
this transformation is taking a long time.

I am curious why it is so hard to accomplish.
I know what it is to manifest with ease.
I have had times in my life
when the weight, the heaviness
slips off
and I move freely.

Oh, how I celebrate those times!
Inside lined up, no conflict
all forward with intentions.

I have been learning some deeper lessons.
It has been dark down here,
and I can't exactly tell you what I'm doing.
In this place I don't have the luxury
to tell myself what I'm doing.
Eagles and leopards in my dreams,
but in the world manifest,
it is all about the worm.
No eyes, no complex intellectualities.
All sensation.
Guiding.

I am completing a cycle.
It has been a challenging journey,
and oh, how I long for the sun.

Some days are meant for rest,

so much digging and digesting.
So I rest
in the dark
with the weight of the world
all around me
and in my heart
hold to the knowing that spring comes,
and dream
that maybe through all of these changes,
I will be given wings,
and just like the gentle butterfly,
take lightly to the sky.

Be Patient with the Healing

Be patient with the healing.

What took decades, centuries, even lifetimes
to set into place
is being unraveled in months and years.
What a change we are making,
and it must be done through our lives.

Instead of stopping the flow
by holding muscle, by holding breath,
hold hands, hold bodies, hold dreams,
and let the current spiral.

Be patient with the healing.

You are so used to pushing and pulling
the body around,
your body, the body of the people,
the body of the earth,
to fit the ideas of the mind.

If you cultivate presence
so many problems are solved.

But, in the chaos of the changing,
it takes immense patience
to sit steady in yourself,
to listen
and truly dialog with "what is,"
to face the requirements
of what the dialog reveals,
to move
knowing the purity of your intentions,

to remain gentle but unbending
while so much falls away.

Be patient with the healing
for the old must always give way
to the new.
And, as in your dreams and visions,
this new self,
this new culture,
this new world,
they are being constructed one moment at a time
in the cycling oneness of our lives.

❧ *Your Life is a Masterpiece* ❧

Spark of Desire

True North

Making my way in the world,
it is pleasing to find
the tools that I have used to find my way
have changed from what I should choose
to what I love to choose.
The inner poles of my being shift,
and what was true north
is no longer true.

The compass becomes guided by longing.

Celebrating in the freedom
of this reformed guidance system,
I skip along and run right into
the requirements of the path.
A little stunned,
first, because in this new partnership with freedom
I did not see the requirements coming.
And, secondly, as I become familiar with
the dialog of freedom,
the directives are never what I think they will be.

The partnership with freedom is an exchange.
It is a two-way street.
It is a mirror
acting as a reflection outside of me.
But, its origins are from within.
Longing, asking, is in itself magic.
And, freedom answers
with its own potent questions,
true to the mirror that it is.
It's necessities usually come from the shadows,
a place inside,

a quality asking to be revealed, unwound, or
developed,
to deliver your longing to you.

When you are no longer bound to old training,
you become deeply bound
to breathing paradox.
No longer operating with blinders and straight lines,
you can relax into the mobility of
inspiration, expiration,
and your life becomes an essential dance,
deeply guided from the inside,
a constant, reflected movement of
bidding, attention, and refinement
beautifully reflected on the outside.

The Valuable Spark of Desire

Don't we get a bit confused by desire?
We chase it, and it is so fleeting,
we are left frustrated with ourselves, with the world.
So, we set out to subdue or control it.

How do you control desire?
Like trying to organize shifting sand,
or commanding ocean waves to stop.

Desire is the natural movement
of our longing,
dancing us into ourselves.

If you trace desire back to its beginnings
is it not born in a spark of inspiration?
A moment when something has your complete
attention and touches you with awe?
A moment when you have allowed
the essence, the power, the beauty of some thing
to affect you deeply?

This is a beautiful thing, this touching, this affecting.

Doesn't the trouble start
when we try to hold to the object of desire?
The object is only the temporary home
of this moving, fleeting brilliance.

Be mindful with the fire.

Tethering yourself

to every shiny object ends in slavery.
But, do not be fooled
into discarding
the valuable spark of desire.

Exactly What You Want

What is it to ask for exactly what you want,
exactly, precisely,
attention to detail
yet not heavy handed?

How many of us go charging off towards
our heart's desire without feeling it through?

Instinct and perception, the Art of feeling it through,
like a fine-tooth comb,
deciphering mixed messages, refining choices,
and discarding feedback that might
sway us away from ourselves.

Untangle and unwind anything that binds you!

It sounds so good, yet
it takes immense courage to refuse to be bound
by the trappings and rules of a social system.

Freedom is truth, your truth.
Do not abandon yourself
out of fear of being branded selfish.
You are an individual self, by nature you are selfish.
Don't be fooled by all the pious training
that keeps you from the power of yourself.

Create your life exactly how you wish.
And, in the exactness of this creating,
rejoice!

For it is through the eye of the needle of self
that true, aligned generosity spills forth, and
the fullness of Life is made manifest.

The Gap of Wanting

Desire:
the gap of something missing,
the in-breath of yearning, looking for a yes.

This is good.

This gap gives us an opportunity
to root for ourselves,
to magnetize others to purpose.

A place
to develop
the storyline of our lives,
intersecting,
weaving
spider webs
together.

We are united in our desire
even if opposing outcomes
are sought.
In the game of creation unfolding
we share the gap.

Please yourself in the wanting.

It is as natural
as your flowing veins,
the minute fraction of a second
when the body says
"More blood" before the next heart beat.

It is the flowers before dawn
quiet and craning

for the earth to turn
one more degree
to bask in the sun.
It is the look in your eyes
to see if you will be met
with love.

Notice the gaps.
Know their magic.
Expand your ability to drop further
into the abyss
of creation.

What Do I Need?

What do I need?
Magic words.
A key hidden under years of training,
blankets of morality suffocating true searching
saying "Too selfish, don't go near."

Where do you go to experience the world
if not through the self?
How do you experience the world
if not through your own swaying of equilibrium?

"What do I need?"
Like checking the rudder on calm days,
or, in a storm taking down the sails
and pulling in tight.
I have been that ship
thrown about on the outer sea,
believing it too selfish
to tend to my own systems,
apologizing for being on the water.

It is the same how I have walked
on grass, with every footstep
muttering "sorry, sorry, sorry."
It is a relearning
how possibly the grass needs to feel me as much as
my feet need to feel its cool texture,
that it is an exchange,
a nourishing connection
that my needing leads to.

The Shifting Sands of My Desire

I have foolishly
tried to understand
the shifting sands of my desires.
When relishing in the sheer beauty
of what did not exist,
becoming a pattern
then disappearing again,
takes my breath away.

It took a long time
to love this desert.

Always in awe
but a slight shying away,
a distaste
for something seemingly barren
but loaded with power.

I sit in potent solitude.

The sun rises, the sun sets
with red mountains in the distance.

A path waits for me,
timing is everything,
footprints, then swept away, so is
the impermanent nature
of shifting sands.

Go Towards Beauty

On the Journey

Some people on the journey are
so gentle and undramatic that
they slip through the cracks.
They started out beating their chests,
laying out impressive dreams,
then, due to life's experiences,
withdrew into gentleness.

If, at heart, you are a chest beater,
and you know you are meant for bigger things,
then sooner or later
the dam breaks
and all of your
beautiful, smelly, tangled
half-put-together bigness
spills out of the tight packaging.

Extraordinary chaos
is the base camp
some of us are brave enough to rest at
while establishing new resources,
surveying the terrain,
eyeing the summit,
on the way to freedom.

Remember to Rest

Momentum gaining,
stakes played higher,
fine tuning a must
to stay in the center point,
to run smoothly.

As speed accelerates,
impeccably in center,
there is no friction
in the mind
or in the playing field.

Remember to rest.

In the excitement,
it is so easy to get revved up,
to begin to expect
things to go a certain way,
and magnetized in attachment,
even just slightly,
is enough
to pull the whole vehicle
off track.

Sit back.
Remember to rest
by laughing at the
"importance"
of where your mind takes you.
The tendency
is to push and pull.

Sit back
in the silent, explosive magic

of center point.
Right here, right now
perfect fit.

Your impeccable presence
is the key.
And, engaged,
the speed of light
is effortlessly yours.

Remember to rest
and all that mental push and pull
seems so rudimentary.
It is easy to forget.
The mental current is strong.

Remember to rest
and your natural instincts
in manifesting
will not become agitated
but will settle
into their rightful place,
eyes open, soft
ready.

What is the Quality of Your Presence?

Are you here,
right here, right now?

Is your mind trailing behind
in the past
trying to resolve or better something
that has already occurred?

Is your mind racing,
multitasking,
juggling the present
while your sight is set elsewhere,
reaching for the future?

For a moment,
feel your body,
relax your teetering posture,
and align
in a balanced spine.

Take a few breaths here and trust
that the meeting will occur between
your desires and reality.
Let your living be stable
by being in yourself.

What if your desires meet reality
and you're not there to enjoy it?

It happens all of the time.

What is the quality of your presence?
What is the quality of your presence?

We are out of practice
but have expectations of mastery.
It is easier than you think,
but it cannot be bypassed;
it cannot be faked.

Relax,
be present,
and feel.

Questions open, expand. Answers reveal.
Off kilter spinning slows, vision repaired.
Breath expands, unveiling
the bigger picture
of here and now.

Making New Bridges

I am making new bridges
from the island of my mind out into the sea of the
unknown.

Before awakening to how vast life's unfolding,
I thought the landscape of my mind was all that
existed,
tightly muscled, efforting through.

As perception and possibility
expand,
it is striking to me
how entrained to limitation and habit
the mind is.

But, I am patient.

Sometimes it is slow progress
making new bridges,
throwing rope,
setting posts,
mind to heart to soul,
mind to heart to soul.

The mind must be connected.
It carries immense value.
A steady mind,
flexible but still, without friction,
a sleek vessel that cuts through the waters of
existence,

precise,
and leaves no wake.

If, in the work
of building bridges,
you are going to make waves,
let your heart drive you, be dynamic.
Let the imprint of your joy
jostle the world
and leave a legacy
of generosity and kindness.

Check Your Motives

Check your motives,
maintenance,
like checking your oil,
assessing your tires,
aligning the synchronicity of your firing pistons.

If you have questions of
what road you're on,
question what's driving you.

Check your motives.
How often we wonder
"Why did things fly helter skelter?"
"How did they go awry?"

As you pull back the bow,
know that the arrow will fly
exactly in the direction
of your true aim.

Check your motives.
If you want love,
then begin all action
deep in the motivation of love.
If you want joy,
then coil and ride the wave of joy
that already pools inside you.
If you want success,
then don't let doubt sway you
and begin from the still point
"now"
where you already exist in perfection.

Check your motives

again and again
looking for the absolute truth.
Forgive yourself for your human tendencies
and celebrate the sweetness
of the bullseye's hit.

Check your motives
until you know yourself so well
there is no need to check anything anymore.

Our lives are creative masterpieces,
and more important
than method applied, time invested, and tool used,
is the original spark
of our true aim.

Become the Key

From the moment of your brilliant conception
you have been nurtured and shaped
by life force
endlessly unfolding
inside of you.

As nutrients turned to flesh,
fruits of the garden to the fire of synapse,
oxygen and sunlight constructing
and reconstructing again,
think the vessel that you are!

Filled with emotion and stretching with intention,
what a miraculous accomplishment
this unfolding.

For what purpose has your life been?

To what end these resources used?

A lifetime of in and out
driving you…where?

And your senses!
What of your eyes, ears, and hands?
Has your focus been weighted
on limitation and futility,
or, has it moved with delight like a butterfly,
sampling?
Have you heard the buzzing?
Listen closely.
The sounds are endless "I love you's".

And your hands, your miraculous hands!

Know the power of their doing and undoing,
for they are your imprint upon creation.
Everyday reintroduce your mind to your wise self.
Align your deepest heart of being
with your eyes, ears, hands.
Become the key
that opens
the door to all possibility.

It is good to ask questions:
Who am I? Where am I going?
And, for what end?

But, it is better
to relax so deeply into creation,
the silent roar,
the infinite light patterns,
the inexplicable beauty,
with a silent bow.

You know without a doubt
that you are a perfect fit.

Go Towards Beauty

Go towards beauty.
Do not hesitate.
Do not be embarrassed
when your heart shouts
with delight.

Stretch the places
inside
that hold the familiarity
of limitation.

Spread your wings
full flight
when you wrap me
in your embrace.

Sing
in unsuspecting places.
Shake up
the sleeping world.

Laugh
until nothing hurts
and the light
ricochets and cascades
off your face,
firing your fluid body.

Spark the new healing.
Reap the harvest of love
with your abounding Joy!

❧ *Your Life is a Masterpiece* ❧

Your Life is a Masterpiece

I Look Fucking Great

I look fucking great.
I want to yell it out loud
in this crowded café.

I want to write a love song to my self,
say nice things,
encourage without demanding anything,
shower myself with all the things
I reach for
with bright eyes and a beating heart,
dance with wildness or sensuality, or
sit very still with mischievous eyes
that pool out into the sea of Knowing
so when you look into them you can't help
but dive in and join me.

I want to appreciate every second of my self,
checking my skin for freckles or wrinkles or
scars I never saw before
pointing like a treasure map to the
story that has shaped me.

Listening, setting into motion
the subtle currents of self unfolding,
no doubts, no withholding,
all love and curiosity.

Replacing the relentless pounding
of "not enough," "not enough," "not enough"
with the sweet whisper
"I'm all right."

How Lovely to Live Where Everything Fits

When you tune to the subtle currents
there is a lot of house cleaning to do,
so much bulk to be thrown out
or given away,
a compelling need to move this to there
until it feels just right.

How lovely to live
where everything fits,
where every object is loved,
and has a living purpose,
dead weight begging
to be thrown back into the river
of life's movement.

It is a meticulous process,
no pretending that something broken
isn't in need of repair or shouldn't be discarded.

To move freely
you must make room
and, with great precision and love,
make ruthless choices
as to what
will anchor your existence.

I Would Rather Make Wine of Life

I have died a thousand times
clinging to life.
Breath stops
and muscles go rigid
trying to freeze frame it,
do it over again,
reshape it,
perfect it,
be better.

I am done wrestling the life out of my experience.
I would rather make wine of life.

Each experience juicy and unique,
ripe, picked, squeezed, savored.
Not about perfection,
for it is the mixture of all these flavors
that makes the wine sweet,
an elixir to be shared with friends
as we sit around smiling,
saying "That was a good year."
 "Aged well."

Let Your Joy Set You Free

Laughing,
cackling, chortling,
giggling, guffawing,
roaring, rolling,
sides aching!

Go ahead, breathe deep and shake out the sheets.

Don't worry about showing the world
what a fool you can be.
Your missteps are so much more life-filled and
interesting than being in control.

It is never too late to loosen up.
Rigidity is fast friends with embarrassment.
Why take anything personally
and add brick and mortar
to life's bondage?

Shake it off, dance it off, tumble the walls
with your bellowing.
Tip the wine and moan
for the food's delightful taste.

Birth new singing ensembles
at every possible occasion.
Spin tales of truth and inspiration.

And, for god's sake, laugh.

Let your joy set you free.

This New Discipline

This new discipline
is subtle in change of pattern,
immense in impact.
The old leaning, spilling out,
transforms in a backward motion
into vessel of self.

What freedom
to move wholly as individual,
the discovery
of "I am"
reflected
in the momentary choices
made over a lifetime.

This new discipline
abolishes blame
and knows responsibility
for what it is,
not a burden to carry for some ideology,
or yoke to wear for membership
into important clubs,
or piece of oneself to trade in exchange for love.

This Response Ability, Response Ability,
is the new discipline to create
freely, fully
the masterpiece of a life.

Your Life is a Masterpiece

Self love,
a catchy phrase,
overused advice,
its importance lost sometimes.

Self love,
simple in its true application,
profound in its effect,
a daily dialog of listening and gentleness
that prepares the ground
for wild and tasty things to grow,
unbending awareness to guard one's resources,
a fierceness that rises from the belly
to care for the fragile
incubation of personal creation.

Your life is a masterpiece.
Your mindfulness,
the vitality and precision that shapes it.

Your self love,
the absolute requirement
nourishing its possibility.

Your Life is a Masterpiece

About the Author and Artist

Rebecca Folsom is a singer, songwriter, touring performer, and fine artist. She has released five CDs and is currently in the studio producing her sixth. She received a Bachelor of Fine Arts from the University of Colorado and has exhibited her paintings in numerous galleries.

Rebecca teaches workshops on songwriting and the Art of Vocal Freedom at retreats and music festivals across the United States. *Sliver* and *Your Life is a Masterpiece* are her first poetry books. Born and raised in Boulder, CO, Rebecca lives in the foothills of the Rocky Mountains.